This purchase
was made
possible
with the
Peyton Funds.

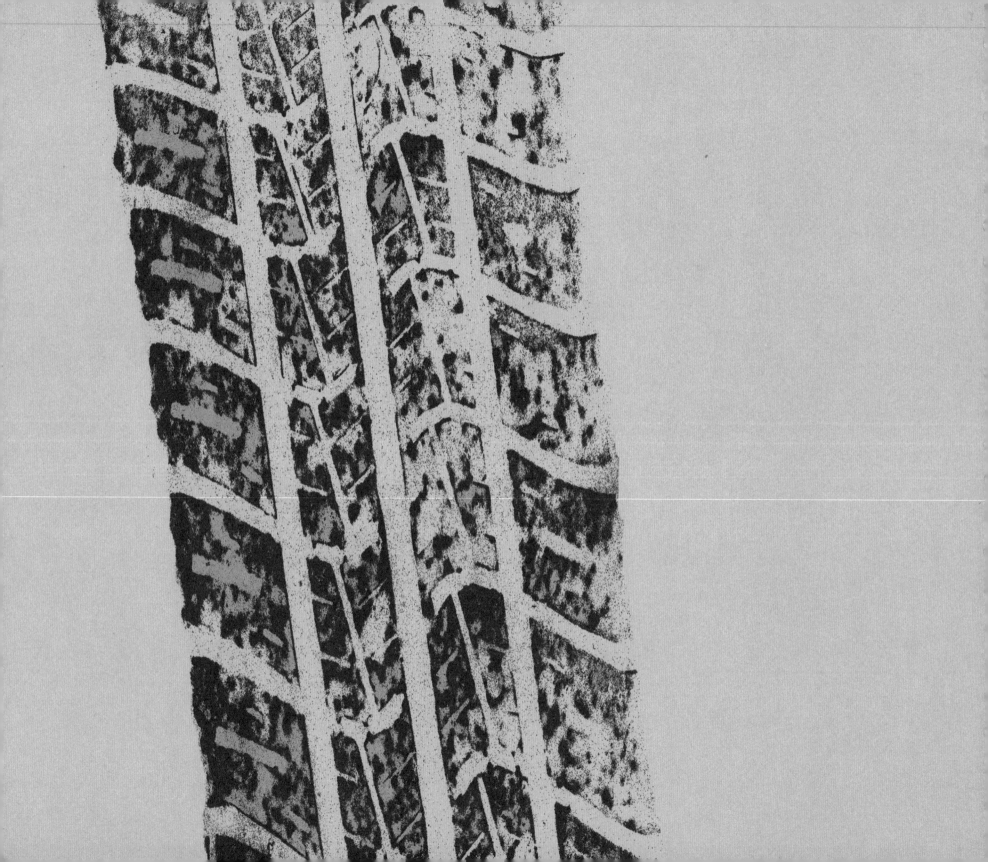

I DRIVE A SEMITRUCK

by Sarah Bridges

illustrated by Derrick Alderman & Denise Shea

PICTURE WINDOW BOOKS
Minneapolis, Minnesota

Thanks to our advisers for their expertise, research, and advice:

Laura Crackel, Managing Editor of Overdrive
Tuscaloosa, Alabama

Susan Kesselring, M.A., Literacy Educator
Rosemount-Apple Valley-Eagan (Minnesota) School District

Managing Editors: Bob Temple,
    Catherine Neitge
Creative Director: Terri Foley
Editors: Brenda Haugen,
    Christianne Jones
Editorial Adviser: Andrea Cascardi
Designer: Nathan Gassman
Storyboard development:
    Amy Bailey Muehlenhardt
Page production: Banta Digital Group

The illustrations in this book were
rendered digitally.

Picture Window Books
5115 Excelsior Boulevard
Suite 232
Minneapolis, MN 55416
877-845-8392
www.picturewindowbooks.com

Library of Congress Cataloging-in-Publication Data
Bridges, Sarah.
I drive a semitruck / by Sarah Bridges ; illustrated by Derrick
    Alderman and Denise Shea.
p. cm. — (Working wheels)
Includes bibliographical references and index.
ISBN 1-4048-0616-4 (reinforced library binding : alk. paper)
1. Tractor trailer combinations—Juvenile literature. [1. Tractor
    trailers. 2. Trucks.] I. Alderman, Derrick, ill. II. Shea, Denise, ill.
    III. Title. IV. Series.
TL230.15.B75 2004
629.224—dc22
                                            2003028228

3

My name is Tyler. I drive a semitruck
for a big trucking company.

My truck hauls things from one place
to another. I take long and short trips.

Semitrucks carry everything from cars and feathers to computers and artwork. Some trucks are even refrigerated so they can keep food cold.

5

My truck is **huge!** It's longer than one and a half school buses. When it's fully loaded, it weighs more than eight elephants!

Semitrucks have 18 wheels to balance the weight of the truck.

I turn the key. The engine starts with a *growl*, and the cab *shivers*.

My seat is very *soft*. It feels like a *comfy* living-room chair.

The cab of the truck is insulated, which makes it quiet for the truck driver.

My truck has a special computer in it.
I put a data card into the computer
when my day starts.

The computer keeps track of where I go and how fast I drive.

At the end of the driver's day, the data card sends information from the truck to a bigger computer at the trucking company's office.

11

I drive my truck short or long distances to deliver the cargo.

My semitruck has a compact disc player and air conditioning. These items make my trip a lot more fun.

I drive more than 1 million miles before my truck is replaced. That's like driving across the United States 333 times!

Trucks receive regular safety checks to make sure everything is working well.

My semitruck also has a special
radio called a CB.

My CB lets me talk to other truckers as we drive.

Drivers also use their CBs, or citizens-band radios, to warn others about dangerous road conditions and bad weather.

My truck has other special instruments inside the cab, too. Dials show me the truck's air pressure, water temperature, and oil pressure.

Drivers do a safety check on their trucks at the beginning and end of each day.

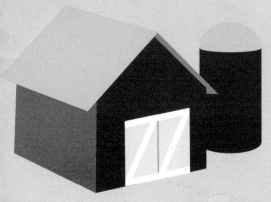

As I drive my truck, I see small towns, **big** cities, *dusty* fields, and grazing cows.

I watch out for problems on the road, too. If there is an accident, I call the police and stop to help.

Some drivers are part of a highway-watch program. They are trained by the highway patrol to help keep the roads safe for everyone.

19

Even when my trip is done, I still have work to do. I check to make sure my truck is in good shape. Then it is ready for the next trip.

Each driver fills out a report at the end of the day. The report lists things that need to be fixed on the truck.

SEMITRUCK DIAGRAM

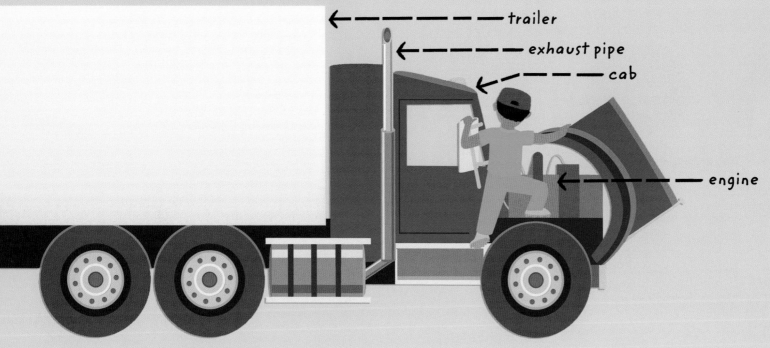

trailer

exhaust pipe

cab

engine

GLOSSARY

cab—the front of the semitruck where the driver sits; the cab is separate from the trailer that holds the cargo

cargo—the items carried by a truck

citizens-band radio—a radio used by truckers to talk to one another while they are driving

data card—card that goes into the semitruck's computer and stores all the information about the truck's trip; it's about the size of a library card

exhaust—the waste gases an engine makes when it is working

FUN FACTS

 Laws require that drivers stop to rest every 250 miles (400 kilometers). Many roadside restaurants are called truck stops. They provide places for truckers to take a break and relax. Truck stops also have bigger parking spaces for the trucks.

 Some semitrucks have a sleeping compartment behind the driver's seat. This gives truck drivers a nice place to rest at night.

 It takes longer for a semitruck to stop than for a car to stop. For that reason, semitrucks stay farther behind the vehicles in front of them.

 The exhaust from a semitruck pours out of a special pipe that looks like a chimney. If there is a lot of black smoke coming from the exhaust pipe, it may be a sign the truck is having engine trouble.

 The driver does not need to type in words on the truck's computer. Instead, the driver just touches the screen to work the computer.

TO LEARN MORE

At the Library

Lipschultz, Jeremy Harris, and Stan Holtzman. *Classic American Semi Trucks*. Osceola, Wis.: MBI Publishing Co., 2000.

Mitchell, Joyce Slayton. *Tractor-Trailer Trucker: A Powerful Truck Book*. Berkeley, Calif.: Tricycle Press, 2000.

Stille, Darlene R. *Big Rigs*. Minneapolis: Compass Point Books, 2002.

On the Web

FactHound offers a safe, fun way to find Web sites related to this book. All of the sites on FactHound have been researched by our staff. www.facthound.com

1. Visit the FactHound home page.

2. Enter a search word related to this book, or type in this special code: 1404806164.

3. Click on the FETCH IT button.

Your trusty FactHound will fetch the best Web sites for you!

BOOKS IN THIS SERIES
- I Drive an Ambulance
- I Drive a Bulldozer
- I Drive a Dump Truck
- I Drive a Garbage Truck
- I Drive a Semitruck
- I Drive a Snowplow

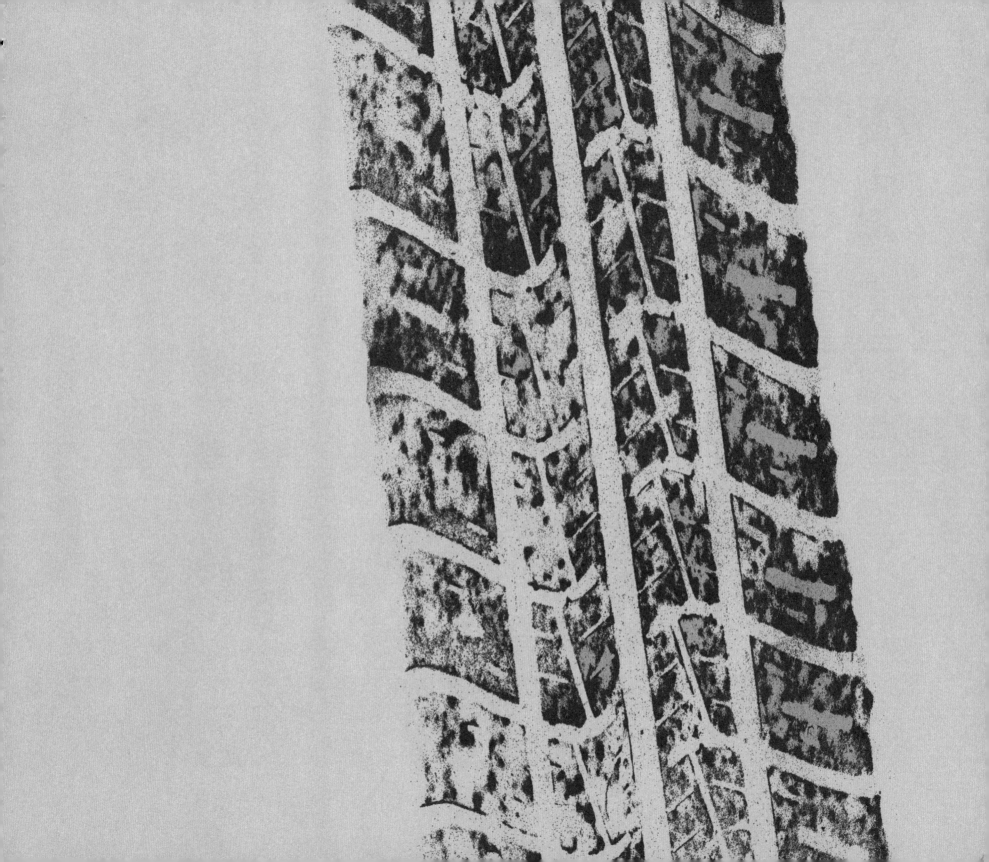